Ghosty Boo

It is love that drives this poetry, a love that lets the intelligence of the neglected glimmer and beat and breathe and crackle. *Ghosty Boo* circles through the magic and myth of a child raising her hand in the air, hoping a bird will land there. Here, Litterer stands up and offers us a talisman for walking in trauma, offers us talons.

-Kelin Loe, author of *These Are the Gloria Stories*

Ghosty Boo lives inside of a book by Kate Litterer who lives with "a hard job to hurt out of revolted love." Poetry is always asking us what is it we're willing to do, and when we take into our own private worlds what's sincere and true, fierce and relentlessly unforgiving are we able to ever feel safe again? *Ghosty Boo* has an answer for that.

-Dara Wier, author of *You Good Thing*

This is a sometimes harrowing, sometimes raunchy, and always gripping book that chronicles abuse, neglect, and trauma. Don't open the cover expecting poetic transcendence. *Ghosty Boo* is that rare book of unmitigated frankness. It casts a cold eye on the world and on the self and in so doing creates a memorable, puissant darkness.

-Lynn Emanuel, author of *The Nerve of It: Poems New and Selected*

Ghosty Boo

Kate Litterer

Cover photograph by Stephen Welch
Cover design by Ryan W. Bradley
Book layout by Walter Bjorkman

Copyright: ©2016 Kate Litterer

ISBN-13: 978-0692507421 (A-Minor Press)
ISBN-10: 0692507426

First Edition, A-Minor Press

for my sister, Amy

Some poems in *Ghosty Boo* have appeared in or are forthcoming from Coconut, Dusie, Finery, Forklift, Ohio, h_ngm_n, La Vague, Spoke Too Soon, and Quaint.

I would like to extend thanks to the following people who supported my poetry and helped me give Ghosty Boo a voice in this collection.

My chosen family. My biological family. My sister. My good lover. My best friend. My femme witches. The editors and mentors who have supported and shared my poetry. And finally, the feminist and queer poets whose words changed me and empowered me.

Contents

Break

Before I RAN THE STREETS MAKING OUT way before I had never witnessed an accident car or beating hurt someone badly enough they might perish so when we were visiting family in Arizona I was probably 8 we drove around curly turns like a family WE SPED UP CANDYLAND MOUNTAIN we passed a bicyclist against the mountain wall covered in BLOOD I WAS A VIRGIN SO it was like being reverse-christened or maybe he had been covered with a blue tarp the cops were there talking and writing like vultures on clipboards it was the early nineties some adults have big dogs for petting SOME MEN HAVE NICE BIG houses later that day I fiddled with a hand-held cooler spigot thinking it was soda and beer filled my two-ounce mouth and I swallowed it MAYBE THE BIKER WASN'T DEAD YET the adults were somewhere I bet it spilled down my chin down my little lace chest JUST HURT REAL BAD if someone attacks a woman I will murder him no sweat like I WONDER WHY like I AM SHIT AT SLEEP so I stay up focusing my vision on the furniture in her bedroom A GHOST PASSING THROUGH I close my eyes and a man appears she is then underneath him on the wood floor on her knees I USUALLY STAB HIM REPEATEDLY IN THE BACK with a kitchen knife but sometimes I crush his head in from the side WITH A BASEBALL BAT I END by kicking him in the gut sometimes this loops until I pass out

At any moment women
might have to rally
individually to lose a piece of our bodies.
To a butcherman.
No one knows my sacrifice
except me and my bone-taker.
Tell me the difference
between stealing
and giving.
I assume it's rule-based and up to ranking.
I bicker like I have always crackled
in a fire pit.

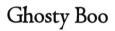

Ghosty Boo

I was suicidality. It sounds
like potentiated
seesaw: I might leave
the house and look
to my neighbors, market-
bound. I might make
it through another day,
then another.
I am sawing
inside trees down.
The trees are howling
and pissing themselves
with fear.

Ghosty Boo brushes my
hair from my face and coos.

Games I played as a child
were twisted off
the cob: violence
portioned in little hands.
Hiding in clothes hampers
tucked like birds,
sucking it in to protect
was to play. I am surprised
we didn't bite
other kids at school. I fall
in love with therapists
and the thought of cutting
off their smile rays and
endorphin and serotonin
showers brings me
dark blues. I want to
make them Christmas gifts
and handwrite long letters.

Come here, Ghosty Boo.
I have questions I want to ask you.
You are so fierce, little fire spit.

But no one knowns me!

Ghosty Boo is part little
girl, part monster. Ghosty
Boo has a vacuum
for a face. Sometimes it's
a pansy bat throat
dripping.

Her favorite times:
being a child ghost forever,
invisibility, screeching,
cuddling up, sucking teddies
like a fucking magnet,
masturbating,
skipping around, songs
about boys, cleaning up glass,
microwaving,
catching worms,
remembering dead
animals, and accidents.

Ghosty has complex PTSD,
she just doesn't know yet. I have
complex PTSD that manifests in hyper
vigilance. Super hereing.

Ghosty molests
herself due to severe neglect.

      Why does it have to be that: molestation?

A therapist told me
severe childhood neglect mirrors symptoms
of child sexual
abuse, Ghosty Drew.

There is a bat in the room.

Thwacking the eaves.
Ghosty Boo erects in bed, bat
bumps and grinds on
the wood. Ghosty Boo is
6 and her eye
sockets crack so her eyes go
owl. Will her parents
notice the subtle
animal shift?

Someone maleish removed
the bat. Ghosty Boo had a little
computer who talked to her
under the blanket.
She had a huge IQ at 5
because her brain
stretched so wide to catalogue:

> *barn, bat, touch,*
> *fiber, wood, hurt, high,*
> *low, snake, thigh, pig,*
> *rabbit, honeybee, dark,*

> *crackle.*

Who killed Ghosty? Who shut
her and filled her with an ocean
of booze?

> *What is this? I try to shake it off*
> *by vibrating my entire body but I am*
> *coated.*

Ghosty blinks in and out horror
girly when I trigger.
Not now, go to sleep go, rest go
go. It's okay, girly boo.

My father lassos
snake necks with white
twine looped on a stick,
jerking his wrist
like starting a
chainsaw. He cuts snakes
thick like butter, says snake
tongues hear like little girls'
ears, then tugs mine. Once.
Each. I clamp down
on bumblebees
with clothespins, plunk
their dizzy bodies in a mason
jar. My sister and I pop
fireflies on the concrete, and
smear until the juice
runs out.

The first time I was stung,
I landed palm down in the grass,
needled. Bee punishment
sudden. Did I cry, little sting?
I mother the spiders.
Little asexual mothers
are we.

I remember
killing, but not
what happened
to the bodies. Just
jars of dead?
Who disposed?
Who shushed?

Ghosty Boo is angry and throbbing threats.
I waver and flicker vision.

Little me is waiting
in the next room for me to
acknowledge her
existence. She has
red poker hair and little
arms and legs and girl
girl voice. Little girl me opens
her mouth and it keeps
going deep and black
and vicious and empty.
Little neglected me
is frozen. She blinks out
then in, horrorific babygirl.
Little me is crying, adult me
watched my own neglect like
a magic zipper closed it.
I drunk to grow up little me
to a sexpot. Little me was a dinky
plastic flower. I close my tight
mouth and I ignore little me. She is
imagined broke fledgling. Me me here,
a panic. Me is closing my mouth
and it keeps going. It is deep
and pink and pulsing like a vagina.

My little vagina is pulsing
like a mutant. Little alien me.
My little vagina is too big and loud, my
me me is too girl horror keeps opening
and spilling. We survive.

I breathe deeper. I breathe

shallower.

She cannot possess me. She only can emit.

Say When

A group of ladies reading poems
is called a vagina reading or so
I have heard from men.
Scene: touch my fashion show
I baked you a cake
shhhh check out the mood lighting
I wore my nasty panties
I shined my hips I washed my hair.

This one is called
PUT YOUR
FAT FINGERS UP MY SKIRT

please?

CUT to me furious
stilting on hard calves in need of massage
my hair is dirty, it smells like old clothes + taffy
oh my it is sexy when a queer woman bites her nails
down to the bloodcomingout.

It's a hard job to hurt out of revolted love.

The lights in my queer bar don't have eyelids.
I bolted them to the ceiling before you came.
What do you call a group of queers
in the Midwest doing nasty love?

A) reinforcement

B) one's on deck watching out

C) we have to take turns sucking face

D) who gives a fuck what you think

      SHE'S SO HOT I KNOW RIGHT?

because I love you I will not kill myself

When I call myself a fag, you wince.
I name myself a rat, I'm poor it helps me think
gooder. I will be your sexy rat whether you like
or no.

How do I know when to say when?

WHENWHENWHEN I walk

say parking lot say graduate class say clinic say
bills say sweat say despair say bat your eyes
say my eyes under batting are my FETISH
the work boots of Butch Daddies
are my angels. Say my angels. Say angels. Say my name.

Obviously I greed
and you look so good
and you watch out for me while
you watch out for yourself.
I censor my words because I use your mouth to speak from.
Fish fist. I put words in your wet lady mouths.
I am projecting and isn't that
so sad like an animal in a zoo?

I want you to walk on me
we should take turns
walking on each other
to make physical the inside walked-on we feel
when women bauble into gay bars in Ohio for
bachelorette parties and we stop and look up in fear
because I want to
slap her her her head
while you licked that pretty envelope
in your sleep I wet my face
trying to lick my black eye.

I called my mother to tell her about you,
bachelorette in the gay bar in Ohio
I told her I was *so angry* and she quieted.
When my lover gets angry she shakes
quiet but I will not kill anyone I will
poach in hot hot water I will wish you
barren. I leave terrified of myself.

Terror Rooms

Three crows flew
over me in a triangle today,
carrying an invisible flag
between them, floated,
then expanded. I
had to follow them
one at a time. Like an owl.

Crows can see the past,
present, and future. Well, I can't
see my fucking past, present,
and future at the same time, Ghosty
Boo, girly boo, and I am
sick because you grew up and
in like a hangnail stem
off a plant curled up
in her swollen survival sac.
Invented your own placenta
like a pumpkin, to nourish
you need inside and
nibble. Ghosty beats against my
body like I am her trap.
She stands across the room and howls
and foams electrically.

Dedicated Ghosty Slueth
dons her cigarette. She is 12.

> *It is just addition and subtraction. Take one*
> *kiss from your mom,*
> *then tie it to reactions years later:*
> *crossing her face out*
> *of your private albums with*
> *RED LIPSTICK. The lips!*
> *The tongue.*

Ghosty Boo bows
unfortunately.

This is a top-down mechanism
with magical animals
that photobomb
my subconscious to shake down
murky answers.
The goal is to feel sad
for Ghosty Boo and dig dirt.
Leave me new but not
baby fresh.
I don't know if I'll ever feel safe
with babies.

Sleuuuuuth!
Sleuth and ye shall find!
Let's make it a memory
game: who can remember most
terse physical. BINGO!

I remember:
being slut-shamed pre-
pubescently.
That word: slut; being afraid
of all men, assuming they'd
beat me and tie me up
and leave me like that.

One time, I got stuck in
an elevator with a drunk
bro and I held
my breath all 19
flights up.
One time, I grew
wings
and hooves.

>*Maybe someone dropped you*
>*in an elevator when you were a baby!*

Dropped me on a
dick in an elevator?

Ghosty Boo nods.

I sprouted
talons
in that elevator and every
day since.

Ghosty muses, then bounces.

>*No. No no no, silly. Fear*
>*of sex and fear*
>*of beating are equated;*
>*because you lack*
>*attachment, all touch*
>*is abuse.*

I used to sing
about boys I crushed on.
I'd walk our backland alone
discussing which boys
liked me and feign surprise
to sound polite.
It felt real
good. I made a
lot of marker art
in my bedroom on my
little kid's desk.
A big adult desk lived on
concrete in the basement.
I sat at that desk and
cybersexed with adult
men—my AIM
screenname ended with "05,"
the year I would graduate
from high school.
Neon buzzbait jailsign.
My mom discovered the
minimized cybering window
and told me off the same way
as when I printed out
a pentagram with the phrase
not all girls are good girls.
"you know this
isn't okay? Okay."
When I got my period
at 10, I raided
the prep pack the elementary school

had mailed to all fourth
grade girls. I hid my bloody
cotton underwear beneath the toolshed
to decompose.
So embarrassed of my
pussy and its needs.
When our dog ran away, I'd stay up
praying to God that she would come
home safe. Night was never
still or silent in my terror
home, and if I hear
"Bridge Over Troubled
Water" ever again at 2AM
I will retch tears from my bilebag.

It's fine it's fine it's fine it's fine.

No one is sorry.

I am a machine of practical
work, I bow to the temple
of patterns. I keep
my emotions simmering in a shed,
latched. I do not touch
and cannot be touched. Am level.
I am inherently good,
Ghosty Boo is innocent.

If you touch us, we will simmer
and roll and twitch your
fingers from our skin. We evade like
a karate snake with eyes
bigger than a wolf owl. We teeter
between retrograde and
progression. Ghosty Boo knows
the shame of survival
the way that I know
a balanced food pyramid, not
to touch a stranger's dog
without asking, the smell
of rotting dairy.

Open places of safety:
back yards,
farms, lakes and
ponds, nourishing meals.

Scary, closed:
darkness/nighttime,
showers, mirrors.

Terror rooms:
night terrors about the room
with the thin carpet on
concrete where there are meat
hooks hanging from the ceiling,
sudden fear of being
touched so much that
I revert to preverbal, recurring
dream where
the back yard is covered
with dead dogs.

But when I was little I
used to walk around a lot
and make up stories! Maybe
I've internalized the answering
side. I used to imagine the half-
human bloody crawling
man from *Hellraiser*
mounting the stairs to my bedroom
and splooging bloody pus
on the eggshell carpet.
I used to think offering
my body to be pinched,
burnt, and bobbled was
a key
to the glorious land of love
beyond the doorway.

My parents showed up in the ER room
and I was a weird broken bird mammal.

   almost almost almost almost

Panic trigger:
elevators, men,
suffocation,
riding in a car.
I could only sleep
if my mouth was
touching
my girlfriend's skin.

Who rules? Whose rules?
There are no rules, only guidelines
you say out loud to pretense
order. Bedtime is nine. The bus
comes at seven. Once, I found
a tick in the crevice
of my ear while waiting
for the school bus, was
running my little fingers in
my earlobe and I hit
a bump and ripped it and it
flew. I still carry that disgust.
Escape home to go to school and
there are ticks hiding in you.

Doors are wicked animals,
privacy from bodies, but
how does a lock stand
up to beating and banging?
I was afraid
of everything:
curtains were witches,
stuffed animals
had teeth. I projected fear
onto inanimate objects,
even then I cultivated
chatter. I heard a man
slow talk over
the grandfather clock.
Manifest. Infestation
man. Did I learn to
evade touch by evading it
as a child or by surviving?

I wanted to talk
but everyone
cut me off. At school, I got
punished for saying "fuck."
Who knew? How much
did they know? Won't someone
admit so I know why I
must evade touch?

I crawled and hid.

Kids don't understand drunk,
so parents can do it
all they want. Drunken
responders to my little
pipes. I thought it was normal
to toddle around keg parties.

Who touched me, bumped me, rubbed me, fell on me there?

I remember the food:
pancakes, salsa, meat
and potatoes. I fed myself
Doritos, ham and potato chip
sandwiches, melted chocolate
in the microwave.
Latchkey kid.
One time, my family came
home from a fucked
up vacation and I drank
two-week overdue milk.
Puking and reeling and they fed
me licorice to ease the pain.

Swimming in our creek,
I sat on a broken glass jar
and sliced my asscheek.
I tried to fix it alone,
but when I couldn't stop
bleeding, I asked.
My mom and the neighbor
closed my slice
with a butterfly bandage.
When the bandage was
removed later (how much
later?), it took my skin with it
and since then I've had a
wormy division sign
scar on my ass.
I've laughed about it. Haha.
My sister laughed about it. She
had a divot above her ass and I said
she had two assholes. Haha.
Why did we know each other's
nudity so well? I grew up
with enough knowledge and
shame not to siren, so the voices
wanting to wail pressurized
my head and my eyes glowed
and I solidified.

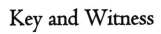

Key and Witness

Last night in a red dress, I observed that
if women are fawns, timid in their drinks, *martini*,
then the man who raped me years ago,
large and barking, is a black wolf,
is a shot of whisky.
He got so close: his breath stank
like a casualty. I turned into an ocean
and sent out tide after tide until
my red flesh dress was a deer's hide
soaked in sea water until the skin
hardened and cracked.

First we were clothed, then under our clothes
naked and painted wide-eyed nude, he
hiding a bottle of liquor and
myself. I camouflaged in black,
my encouragement or fear,
our looping, the sound of trains
translated into barking until I tinkled
like a music box.

If I closed my eyes, I heard trains.
My mother and I watched graffiti roll past
while we smoked, backs on the red brick station.
Red Brick Station is the anywhere in this equation;
we smoked and I quit counting after one hundred.
The man who raped me. One hundred. Mother,
cut off my hair and erase me in parts to leave room.

I am training myself
to be a witch

so healing will be
electric and accumulative.
I hold gems like
precious frogs.

What if I never
connect? What
happens to frog bodies
when they die
inside fish bodies?
My cat tortures
bugs, but I try
to love them when
my hands won't stop shaking.
I need to retire
this body or awaken it.

I try to focus
on rose quartz, rose
infusions. Goddess,
make my blood
rosewater. Please, protect
my deepest beams
and flood my lungs:
larva soup
free me. Fire
pop my cartilage,

Earth, you don't have to soak
in all the ooze
black from abuse.
Let it be
carried away and
repurposed
by insects making homes.

No one knowns me. I cannot
speak. I cannot push
words from my head with my tongue
because my eyes are too wide and my
sockets push my teeth down. I am
afraid of tornadoes inside of the house.
I go outside to play in the mud with my sister.

I keep recreating my relationship
with my sister—caring,
defensive, twinlike, naive,
forgiving—with my adult partners
and it ruins everything.

Gemini weighted Libra.

Once, we posed our Barbie dolls like a Playboy shoot.

>*We stole eggs from the refrigerator*
>*instead of the chicken coop—maybe*
>*we wanted to test if our parents will*
>*notice. They don't.*

Once, my sister threw
my cat into the creek. Once, I threw
a rock in the air knowing it might
fall on her and it did, but I didn't mean it,
I was just curious. The only time
my father spanked me was when I
raced my sister to the front seat of the car,
slammed the door on her fingers, and kept
pulling while she screamed.
I wasn't aware that she was hurting,
was I?

>*But isn't pain regular*
>*and to be expected? Shouldn't my*
>*apology be implied and accepted*
>*without me having to ask for it?*

When you're young and neglected, grotesque
is normal. The floor is lava, you have
a Nintendo, you eat mashed
potatoes, so everything is normal.

I had cybersex with adult men
when I was a preteen. I had horrible
and expected coping
mechanisms starting at age baby.

I never cuddle except to fuck.

I know I owe I owe

Just because those who hurt me
were hurt first
doesn't make it okay.

> *I am innocent*
> *of my crimes but do not realize*
> *I am convicted. I exist as a mouse,*
> *a skank, to turn inside, to*
> *camouflage mixed with attempts*
> *at tenderness, which is an*
> *instinct. I give up, eventually,*
> *on tenderness.*

I owe I owe I owl

Once, I was a teenager and
I lay my head on my father's thigh
while we watched TV. This was my attempt
at normal physicality for a father-daughter
relationship. It felt weird
as fuck and I was embarrassed. You don't
walk up to a stranger
and hug them. You don't
touch your parents sweetly
if you never did before, *crazy*.
Who is this foolbaby?
What does she eat? What does she do
for a living? The foolbaby is beautiful and dimply.
She is a dough pustule!
She is not real.

I haven't had sex
in ages. Kissing is riding a carousel,
leaning out and trying to
grab the metal ring when you circle by.
If you miss, you have a
rotation to harden yourself
until you turn to stone.

My card this year is
Death. Like a flowerbed
tilled and bubbling up, I
stew. I cleanse and hide
under my charcoal
facial cleansing mask.

Terror:
basements, closets from
which evil jumps in
homemade masks,
hags looming,
shrugging it off, dusting
it off, hugging,
laughing to get
to the other side.

My girlself is a pink and white
stuffed poodle in a wicker clothes
basket filled with bears and cats and
little doll people at my therapist's.
I ask good little girl poodle
questions like why
won't you
talk. You are safe here.

Loneliness. Not
eating, being forgotten
to be fed.
I placate so you
wouldn't know I waver
between patronizing and
shock.

My little poodle self
likes to draw
only when others draw with her.
As kids, we made up
a game called
Attack In The Dark.
You had to make it from one
side of the basement to
the home base, but we
shut out the lights
and everyone hid
and jumped out at you.
I remember piecing myself
in a white wicker hamper and shutting
the lid over my head. My

grandfather bought my sister
and me matching
hampers for Christmas and we were
disappointed.

Our games hit
and hurt our growing
bodies. We practiced
violence like no big deal.

     It was fun.
     I think it was fun.

When I was 16,
I fucked like a little porno.
Like the best of them. Getting
hit at 16 is different than
Attack In The Dark.

I dropped the Super Nintendo
controller in a bucket of
water in the laundry room
when I was angry at my sister.
Who was punished by that act?
I would also chew
the cord and my nails and
my shirt sleeves. My sister
punched me in the stomach
once because I wanted to use
the internet. She pushed me
through a screen door because
I kicked the chair she
sat on while using the
fucking internet.
I scraped up bloody, she dusted
off and returned quiet.
To what? To games of fantasy
homes with mommies and daddies
and clean babies?

We named our dog Chelsea
after Clinton.
I remember her flaking
with her mange. She looked
like mold. She festered in
fleas, who popped like
corn. What my parents had to
hide, they burnt in a barrel.
One of my most vivid
love memories is chasing
with my sister and trying to whip
each other with wet
curled up t-shirts. Chelsea
went somewhere, but I can't
remember...

My sister and I murdered a rooster
when we were children. It was on accident.
We found him in our barn. He displayed
himself patiently to our awkward strokes then
started bleeding from his beak slits.
Because my sister and I had never been
so close to a rooster and because we were 5
and 6, we played doctor. I held his beak
while she placed a stone in his mouth.
We switched hands and I placed another small stone
in his mouth. She was older; I loved her and let her
go first. Eventually, the rooster swallowed
or he choked on the stones.
He couldn't entertain; stroking him felt like
stroking a cheap carnival prize.
How were those stones smaller than bees?
How did our girlish hands learn to
dole them like pills and tell the rooster,
"I know it hurts, I'm sorry" without knowing
what it meant to hurt but knowing to
take turns saying, "it's good for you."

When my father won us
in the custody battle, my sister
and I were fledglings again.
We had to detail the dog shit
piles we went to bed and
woke up to, re-live
the flea bites and—
from what I can deduce
from my severe
PTSD dissociation
triggered by
missing dinner—
our lack of feeding.

> *I am not sure.*

I know.
You coped.

What am I making up?

Dear Daddy I keep it together
like crystal clear and trying
at the rock climb wall and the
shining star that I want to be
for you.

This is the hermit year where
I learn how to boil down fats
and flowers to make lipstick alchemy
for me Daddy but also for you.

It feels not
possible to find you
inside of me. The
webs of open shutters
on cabinets.

Daddy have you met my goddesses
they are all eager to test you

stand against the moon
and if your shadow is long
enough they will
rub you with salts
and x-ray you with their ancient eyes.

My goddesses are guiding me
not towards you but myself
like a ship bobbing in the night ocean
and they are my lighthouses
every ten or twenty miles.

It's practice for when they let me
go alone into the night to find
my own signs. No more feathers
found on walks or bird calls
or the bright red crown of the woodpecker.

Daddy I can do many things
always. Break down the carcass
of the chicken for broth,
step one. Love the soft
snaking valleys on my sides,
wash daily, step two. To be a good
girl without a Daddy is what
the goddesses want from me.

Sometimes I treat them like Daddy,
petulant, needing a sign
now. To fall back into
their airy arms is eons harder than
shining the linoleum for
you to inspect Daddy.

The goddesses want me to
learn how to eat meat and feel
the heartbeat in my own chest.

I cannot be waxed, tied,
looked at crooked
without steel walls eking
my skin away. I got
slapped hard in
my face: no one saw.

I have never run so energetically.
Pulsing: quick decider good job.

It makes fucking
difficult
different
death.

I am terrified
like a rescue pup
of disappointing bosses.
I was an office assistant
at a Jewish University Center
all four years in college.
Every Friday, I was
the shiksa who
stayed late to
lock up the beeping
four-digit alarm
system and walk
home in the dark. I got
free dinner, which was necessary
the month I worked
60 hours a week at 2 jobs
and lived on
a combination of bulk pasta,
salty spaghetti sauce,
and cheddar cheese. I called
it "pasta vomit." I ate
a 5 lb. bag of
walnuts for a day or two.
Since then, walnuts are my
kryptonite. One night,
in the middle of a fuckfest with
a sweet husky-eyed
girl I'd met online, I
orchestrated a case of beer

drop off: it cost me $40.
Double the cost of the case.
I couldn't fuck
if I wasn't wasted. I was 20.
She was 18 and struggled
with meth but loved
animals.
We rode the bus
the next day: me to work
with come under my nails and
beer breath. Her down
town and away. It was
more about the fucking plus
the drinking: it wasn't love
unless love for abandonment.
At work, a blind young
Jewish man who talks a lot
rubs his fingers on my desk chair
and sniffs them when those
who came to pray
are praying and I stand
ten feet away.
My eyes fearpopped; I
waited for him to leave.
I threw up
inside my body,
sloshed and produced
venom. I drunkfucked
so many women
that summer. It didn't stop
a big black dick
from flopping
next to me on the bus

or men in trucks
whooping at my ass
between classes
or getting roofied and
pissing myself.
It was a white light summer.

I used to wait
down by the backdoor: dog
in one hand knife
in the other all night
til my girlfriend got home
from second shift.
Senior in high school, I quit
everything.
I heard everything. I felt
everything. I wore her
sweatpants to school and ate
what she fed me.

Butch Daddy you better have big arms and lots of money.

I've been drinking a tea called
"Sweet Water for the Well" to
try to put love inside me easily. I know
it doesn't work like that Daddy
but I'm not above
shortcuts to get to feeling
red or pink again. I stocked
up on rose petals, and the apothecary
asked me if I wanted
red or pink, and I had always
gotten pink to act as healing
from childhood trauma. I asked
her what she thought and she said
pink reminded her of grandmothers.

It is too easy to reconnect with trauma.

I burn sage every day
walking the perimeter of my home
holding the smoking bundle like
a preemptive trophic shield. I clean
my hair with it, I reiki the cats,
I reiki the tea kettle, I reiki my
pillows and the cavity in bed.

Daddy isn't sexy
when you say it
outside of fucking.
To be serious, I
sew our pupils on
a string. Level now.

I dance
like a poodle. I groom,
not make myself up:
I *groom*. Lick.

Make me
a chore list. Make up
your mind. What do you want
for dinner?
I'll quit every
thing to be your stay
at home babywife.

Bees have always been there
for me. Horses have always
been strong and hard
and I have always hunted for
a Daddy to praise me
at every step. Butch Daddies
are patrol teddy bears.
I am a jagger bush. A snapping
turtle beak and love is
a branch I want to eat it,
to teach it a lesson about
Do Not Touch Me.
If a Butch Daddy leased
my neck I could go lax and burble.
I would traipse pony-style.
I would be proud to be
daughtered.
I would maybe
be safe.

Kate Litterer received her MFA in poetry from the University of Massachusetts Amherst Program for Poets and Writers. Her poetry has appeared in or is forthcoming from *Coconut, The Destroyer, Dusie, Finery, Forklift, Ohio, h_ngm_n, Ilk, inter|rupture, Jellyfish, La Vague, Mistress, NonBinary Review, Phantom Limb, Route Nine Literary Journal, Sixth Finch, Spoke Too Soon, Quaint,* the anthology *Please Excuse This Poem: 100 New Poems for the Next Generation,* and the anthology *Hysteria.* She is pursuing a PhD in Composition and Rhetoric at the University of Massachusetts Amherst, where she focuses on queer and feminist historiography, butch/femme experience, and archival research. She lives in Western Massachusetts with her two maine coon cats. Her website is katelitterer.com.

Photograph by Sarah Beth Aspen McAlpine

A-Minor Press
Current and Forthcoming Titles

Sam Rasnake, *Cinéma Vérité*

Mary Carroll-Hackett, *If We Could Know Our Bones*

Michael Keenan, *TRANSLATIONS ON WAKING IN
AN ITALIAN CEMETERY*

Kate Litterer, *Ghosty Boo*

Nate Pritts, *Post Human*

In Memory of Walter Bjorkman (1948-2015)